Maths

Rapid Tests 1

Rebecca Brant

Schofield & Sims

Introduction

This book gives you practice in answering mathematics questions quickly.

The questions are like the questions on the 11+ and other school selection tests. You must find the correct answers.

School selection tests are usually timed, so you need to get used to working quickly. Each test has a target time for you to work towards. Ask an adult to time you.

What you need

- A pencil
- An eraser
- A ruler
- A clock, watch or stopwatch
- A sheet of rough paper
- An adult to time you and to mark the test for you

What to do

- Turn to **Section 1 Test 1** on page 4. Look at the grey box at the top of the page labelled **Target time**. This tells you how long the test should take.
- The adult helping you will tell you when to begin.
- Read each question carefully and then write the answer on the answer line. Sometimes you need to draw your answer in the space instead. You should not use a calculator.
- Try to answer every question. If you do get stuck on a question, leave it and go on to the next one. Work quickly and try your best.
- When you reach the end, stop and tell the adult that you have finished.
- The adult will mark your test. Then the adult will fill in the **Score**, **Time taken** and **Target met?** boxes at the end of the test.
- Turn to the **Progress chart** on page 40. Write your score in the box and colour in the graph to show how many questions you got right.
- Did you get some questions wrong? You should always have another go at them before you look at the answers. Then ask the adult to check your work and help you if you are still not sure.
- Later, you will do some more of these tests. You will soon learn to work through them more quickly. The adult who is helping you will tell you what to do next.

Published by **Schofield & Sims Ltd**,
7 Mariner Court, Wakefield, West Yorkshire WF4 3FL, UK
Telephone 01484 607080
www.schofieldandsims.co.uk

This edition copyright © Schofield & Sims Ltd, 2018
First published in 2018

Author: **Rebecca Brant**. Rebecca Brant has asserted her moral rights under the Copyright, Designs and Patents Act, 1988, to be identified as the author of this work.

British Library Cataloguing in Publication Data. A catalogue record for this book is available from the British Library.

Design by **Ledgard Jepson Ltd**
Front cover design by **Ledgard Jepson Ltd**
Printed in the UK by **Page Bros (Norwich) Ltd**

ISBN 978 07217 1421 9

Contents

A **pull-out answers section** (pages A1 to A16) appears in the centre of this book, between pages 20 and 21. It also gives simple guidance on how best to use this book. Remove this section before the child begins working through the tests.

Target time: **12 minutes**

1. Write the next two numbers in the sequence on the blank beads.

a)

b)
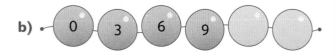

2. What is the value of each underlined digit?

a) 1<u>8</u> _____

b) <u>2</u>8 _____

3. Write these numbers in order, smallest first.

34   12   5   18   22

_____

4. Write **<** or **>** to make these statements correct.

a) 34 _____ 43

b) 25 _____ 27

5. Write these numbers in words.

a) 27 _____

b) 38 _____

6. Write these numbers in digits.

a) Thirteen _____

b) Twenty-eight _____

7. What is the value of the 6 digit in each of these numbers?

a) 26 _____

b) 63 _____

c) 164 _____

8. What is the next odd number after 25? _____

9. Circle the even numbers.

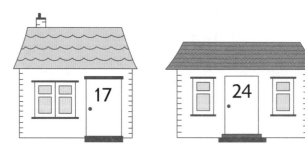

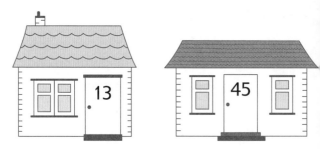

10. Estimate these numbers on the number line.

0   a)   b)   10

a) _____   b) _____

0   c)   d)   10

c) _____   d) _____

Target time: **12 minutes**

1. How many eggs?

+ _____ = _____

2. Write the missing numbers.

a) 6 + _____ = 10

b) 5 + _____ = 10

c) _____ + 3 = 10

3. Solve these calculations.

a) 10 − 2 = _____

b) 10 − 9 = _____

c) 20 − 18 = _____

4. What do I add to 15 to make 22? _____

5. Mya had 11 pencils. She was given 5 more. How many does she have now? _____

6. Henry ran for 13 minutes. He then ran for another 4 minutes. For how many minutes did he run in total?

_____ min

7. Solve these calculations.

a) If 10 + 7 = 17, then 17 − 10 = _____

b) If 6 + 9 = 15, then 15 − 9 = _____

8. Sadie had 12 stickers. Her mum gave her 7 more. How many does she have now? _____

9. Nihal did some maths homework for 10 minutes, then reading homework for 8 minutes. How long did he spend doing his homework? _____ min

10. Write three other calculations that use only these numbers.

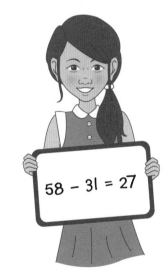

58 − 31 = 27

a) _____ + _____ = _____

b) _____ + _____ = _____

c) _____ − _____ = _____

11. Write the missing numbers.

a) 16 + _____ = 20

b) 12 + _____ = 20

c) 7 + _____ = 20

| Score: | | Time taken: | | Target met? | |

1. Count on in steps of 2.

   a) 0, 2, 4, _____, _____, _____

   b) 16, 18, 20, _____, _____, _____

2. How many cupcakes? _____

3. How many flowers? _____

4. How many spots? _____

5. If there are 10 caterpillars on each bush, how many caterpillars will there be on six bushes? _____

6. What is $\frac{1}{2}$ of 12? _____

7. Solve these calculations.

   a) 2 × 3 = _____

   b) 5 × 8 = _____

   c) 10 × 4 = _____

8. Sadie has 5 bananas in each bunch. If she has 15 bananas, how many bunches does she have? _____

9. Share the apples equally between the two trees.

How many apples on each tree? _____

10. Draw a line to match each sum to the correct set of beads.

   a) 10 ÷ 2

   b) 14 ÷ 2

   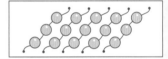

   c) 20 ÷ 5

   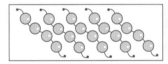

   d) 15 ÷ 5

   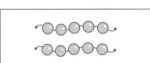

11. Shade the correct fraction of each shape.

   a) $\frac{1}{2}$

   b) $\frac{1}{4}$

   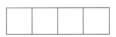

   c) $\frac{1}{3}$

   d) $\frac{3}{4}$

Score: _____ Time taken: _____ Target met? _____

Target time: **12 minutes**

1. Measure the length of these pencils to the nearest centimetre.

a) 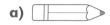 _____ cm

b)  _____ cm

c) 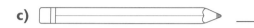 _____ cm

d)  _____ cm

2. John has a piece of wood that is 18cm long. Paul has a piece which is half as long. How long is Paul's piece of wood? _____ cm

3. Match the clocks to the correct times.

a) 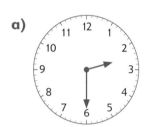 | quarter past 7

b) 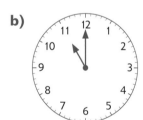 | 11 o'clock

c) 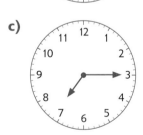 | half past 2

4. Write **<**, **>** or **=** to make these statements correct.

a) 1kg _____ 1000g

b) 1l _____ 1500ml

c) 3m _____ 200cm

5. What is the value of the coins in each purse?

a) 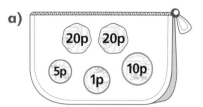 _____ p

b) 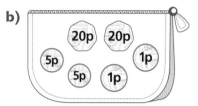 _____ p

c) 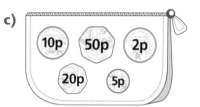 _____ p

d) 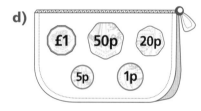 £ _____

6. Convert these measurements.

a) 1000g = _____ kg

b) 3000g = _____ kg

c) 2kg = _____ g

7. How much liquid is in each jug?

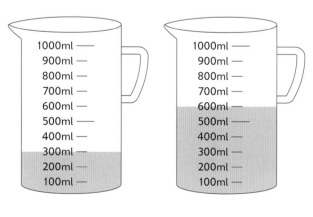

a) _____ ml   b) _____ ml

Score:		Time taken:		Target met?	

Maths Rapid Tests 1

7

Target time: **12 minutes**

1. Complete the pattern.

2. Match the shapes to their names.

    a)

    hexagon

    b)

    octagon

    c)

    rectangle

3. Complete the table.

Shape	Number of sides	Number of corners
Square		
Triangle		
Pentagon		
Hexagon		

4. Use a ruler to draw the line of symmetry on each shape.

    a)   b)

    c)   d)

5. Circle the odd one out.

6. Match the objects to their shape names.

    a)

    cone

    b)
    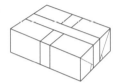

    cylinder

    c)

    cuboid

7. Look at the grid below.

    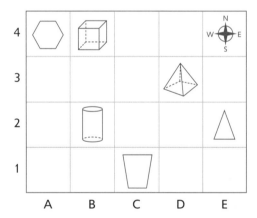

    a) Which shape can be found at B2?

    _____

    b) Where is the square-based pyramid? _____

    c) In what position is the quadrilateral? _____

    d) Which shape can be found directly to the north of the cylinder?

    _____

Score: _____   **Time taken:** _____   **Target met?** _____

Target time: **12 minutes**

1. Sort these numbers into the correct part of the table.

7, 4, 21, 16, 28

Odd numbers	Even numbers

2. The pictogram below shows the pets of the children in Class 2C.

(☺) = 1 child

Dog	☺ ☺ ☺ ☺
Cat	☺ ☺ ☺ ☺ ☺ ☺ ☺
Rabbit	☺ ☺ ☺
Fish	☺ ☺ ☺ ☺ ☺
Hamster	☺ ☺ ☺
Snake	☺

a) How many children had a dog? _____

b) Which two animals did the same number of children have?

_____

_____

c) How many more children had a fish than a snake? _____

d) Two more children got hamsters for their birthdays. How many children have pets now? _____

3. Two children counted the colour of cars in a car park.

a) Complete the tally chart to show the results.

```
W R B S G G Y B B B S
S W W R W B B G P S
W W B G R Y S S B B
B W G G S R B R W W
```

W = White
B = Black
G = Grey
Y = Yellow
R = Red
S = Silver
P = Pink

Car colour	Tally	Total
White		
Red		
Black		
Silver		
Grey		
Yellow		
Pink		

b) Which was the most popular colour?

_____

c) Which was the least popular colour?

_____

d) How many white cars were seen? _____

e) The number of cars that were grey or pink was equal to the number of

_____ cars.

Score: _____ Time taken: _____ Target met? _____

Maths Rapid Tests 1

9

Target time: **12 minutes**

1. Complete these sequences.

   a) 0, 5, 10, 15, _____ , _____

   b) 4, 14, 24, 34, _____ , _____

2. Solve these calculations.

   a) 30 + _____ = 100

   b) _____ + 60 = 100

3. How many minutes are there
   in one hour? _____

4. How many hours are there
   in one day? _____

5. Complete the tally chart below, which shows
   the favourite sports of children in Year 6.

Sport	Tally	Total
Football	ⅢⅢ ⅢⅢ ⅢⅢ ⅢⅢ ‖	
Netball		17
Tennis	ⅢⅢ ⅢⅢ Ⅰ	
Rounders		26
Rugby		15

6. Write these numbers in digits.

   a) Seventy-one _____

   b) Sixty-six _____

7. Sonal drinks half of a 400ml
   bottle of water. How much
   water does she drink? _____ml

8. Hamish the rabbit weighs twice as much
   as Squeak the guinea pig, but half as much
   as Patch the dog. If Patch weighs 4kg,
   how much do Hamish and Squeak weigh?

   a) Hamish _____kg

   b) Squeak _____kg

9. Circle $\frac{1}{4}$ of the toy cars.

10. Draw one line
    of symmetry
    on this shape.

11. Draw the hands on the clocks so they
    show the correct time.

    a) half past 7

    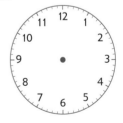

    b) quarter to 5

    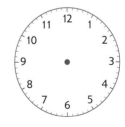

Score: _____ Time taken: _____ Target met? _____

Schofield & Sims

Target time: **12 minutes**

1. Solve these calculations.

a) If 34 + 17 = 51, then 17 + 34 =

_____

b) If 56 + 32 = 88, then 32 + 56 =

_____

2. Find these numbers.

a) What is $\frac{1}{2}$ of 18? _____

b) What is $\frac{1}{4}$ of 20? _____

3. Anya has 20p. She spends 16p.
How much change does she get? _____p

4. Alfie pours 100ml of lemonade into a jug,
followed by 50ml of apple juice.

How much liquid is now
in the jug? _____ml

5. Use a ruler to complete these symmetrical
shapes.

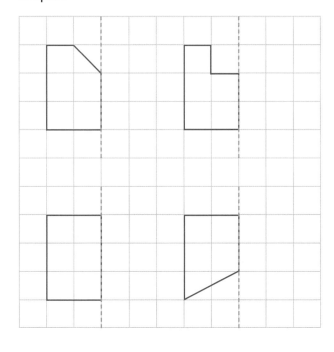

6. Look at the Venn diagram below.

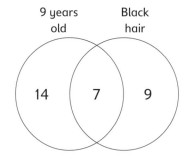

9 years old · Black hair · 14 · 7 · 9

a) How many 9 year olds
were there? _____

b) How many 9 year olds had
black hair? _____

c) How many children were
not 9 years old? _____

7. Jack had 60 marbles. He shared
them between his 10 friends.
How many marbles did he
give to each of his friends? _____

8. Convert these measurements.

a) 100cm = _____ m

b) $\frac{1}{2}$m = _____ cm

c) 2m = _____ cm

d) 4m = _____ cm

9. Jerry was 100cm tall. His brother was twice
as tall, while his baby sister was half as tall.

a) How tall was Jerry's brother? _____cm

b) How tall was Jerry's baby
sister? _____cm

Score:		Time taken:		Target met?	

Target time: **12 minutes**

1. Write these numbers in order, largest first.

   39   26   8   0   22

   _____

2. Write these numbers in order, smallest first.

   56   34   28   11   15

   _____

3. Circle $\frac{1}{2}$ of the sweets.

4. Solve these calculations.

   a) 22 + 6 =   _____

   b) 45 + 30 =   _____

   c) 18 − 5 =   _____

   d) 3 × 2 =   _____

5. What fraction of each shape is shaded?

   a)

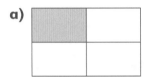

   _____

   b)

   _____

6. What is the value of each underlined digit?

   a) 1<u>6</u>   _____

   b) <u>4</u>5   _____

7. The chocolate bar weighs twice as much as the lollipop. The ice cream weighs twice as much as the chocolate bar. How much do the chocolate bar and ice cream weigh?

   45g   **a)** _____g   **b)** _____g

8. Measure these lines.

   a) ————————————————   _____cm

   b) ——————————   _____cm

9. How much liquid is in each jug?

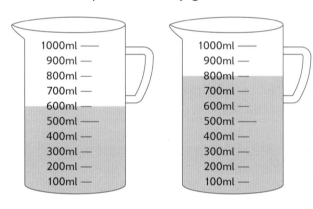

   a) _____ ml   **b)** _____ ml

10. Rocky has 20p. He buys a pencil for 13p. How much money does he have left?   _____p

11. Hannah thinks of a number. She doubles it. The answer is 14. What was her number?   _____

12. Anil thinks of a number. He adds 12. The answer is 22. What was his number?   _____

Score:		Time taken:		Target met?	

Target time: **12 minutes**

1. What is the value of each underlined digit?

   a) 7<u>8</u>   _____

   b) <u>1</u>03   _____

2. Mark ✓ for a true statement and
   ✗ for a false statement.

   a) 10 − 8 = 3   _____

   b) 2 + 18 = 20   _____

   c) 2 + 5 + 8 = 15   _____

   d) 8 × 2 = 18   _____

   e) 80 ÷ 10 = 8   _____

3. What are the measurements on these scales?

   a)

   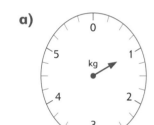

   _____ kg

   b)

   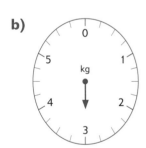

   _____ kg

4. Leila had £1. She spent 20p on a pencil
   and 30p on a pad.

   a) How much did she spend?   _____ p

   b) What was her change?   _____ p

5. Find these numbers.

   a) What is $\frac{1}{4}$ of 8?   _____

   b) What is $\frac{1}{3}$ of 6?   _____

6. Estimate these numbers on the number line.

   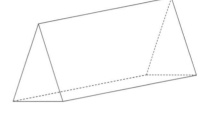

   0 [a)   b)] 10

   a) _____   b) _____

   0   [c)]   [d)]   100

   c) _____   d) _____

7. Name this shape.

   _____

8. The pictogram shows the favourite fruit of
   children in Year 2.

   ☆ = 2 children

Apple	☆ ☆
Orange	☆ ☆ ☆ ☆
Banana	☆ ☆
Peach	☆ ☆ ☆ ☆ ☆
Plum	☆ ☆ ☆
Strawberry	☆ ☆ ☆ ☆ ☆ ☆ ☆

   a) How many children preferred
      strawberries?   _____

   b) How many more children
      preferred peaches than
      bananas?   _____

| Score: | | Time taken: | | Target met? | |

Target time: **12 minutes**

1. Amy bought 5 sweets that cost 9p each. How much did she spend? _____p

2. Circle $\frac{1}{2}$ of the flowers.

3. Measure these lines to the nearest centimetre.

   a) _____ _____cm

   b) _____ _____cm

4. Convert these measurements.

   a) 2000ml = _____ l

   b) 3l = _____ ml

   c) 5l = _____ ml

5. How many lines of symmetry does this shape have?

   _____

6. Xarina had 15 chocolates.

   a) She ate 7. How many did she have left? _____

   b) She then ate another 4. How many are left now? _____

7. There were 18 strawberries in the fruit bowl.

   a) Molly used 7 to make a milkshake. How many were left? _____

   b) She then dropped 2 on the floor. How many are left now? _____

8. Look at these number cards.

   Using these cards, what is the largest two-digit number you can make?

   a) Write it in digits. _____

   b) Write it in words.

   _____

   Using the same cards, what is the smallest two-digit number you can make?

   c) Write it in digits. _____

   d) Write it in words.

   _____

9. The Venn diagram shows what a group of children ate at lunchtime.

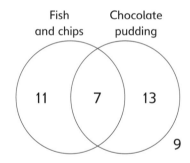

   a) How many children had chocolate pudding for lunch? _____

   b) How many children had both fish and chips and chocolate pudding? _____

   c) How many children had neither fish and chips nor chocolate pudding? _____

10. Ali weighs 21kg. His big brother, Simon, weighs twice as much. How much does Simon weigh? _____kg

Score: _____ Time taken: _____ Target met? _____

Target time: **12 minutes**

1. What fraction of each shape is shaded?

a)

_____

b)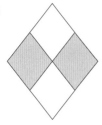

_____

2. Write these numbers in order, largest first.

37 68 21 95 57

_____

3. Write these numbers in order, smallest first.

46 70 38 100 59

_____

4. Kathryn collected 12 stickers. Her friend Louise had collected twice as many. How many had they collected altogether?   _____

5. Solve these calculations.

a) 20 + _____ = 27

b) 16 − _____ = 12

c) 41 + 8 =   _____

d) What must be added to 40 to make 100?   _____

e) What must be taken away from 100 to make 30?   _____

6. Circle the number that equals 8 × 2.

12   16   20   18   19

7. Circle the number that equals 35 ÷ 5.

5   9   3   7   6

8. The block diagram shows the favourite vegetables of children in Class 2A.

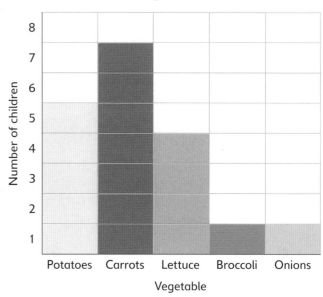

Favourite vegetables of Class 2A

a) How many children preferred carrots?   _____

b) Which two vegetables were liked by the same number of children?

_____

c) How many more children preferred potatoes than lettuce?   _____

d) How many children are in Class 2A?   _____

9. Match the shapes to their names.

a)

| hexagon |

b)

| pentagon |

c)

| quadrilateral |

d)

| octagon |

| Score: | | Time taken: | | Target met? | |

1. What is the value of each underlined digit?

   a) 2̲4 _____

   b) 3̲7̲ _____

   c) 7̲6 _____

2. Write these numbers in words.

   a) 49 _____

   b) 83 _____

3. Write these numbers.

   a) 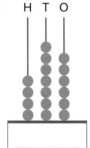 _____

   b) 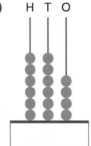 _____

   c) 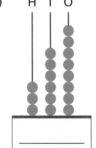 _____

   d) 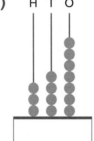 _____

4. List all the even numbers between 45 and 51.

   _____

5. Write **<** or **>** to make these statements correct.

   a) 132 _____ 123

   b) 168 _____ 186

   c) 243 _____ 432

6. Write these numbers in digits.

   a) One hundred and twenty _____

   b) Eighty-two _____

7. Look at these number cards.

   Using these cards, what is the largest two-digit number you can make?

   a) Write it in digits. _____

   b) Write it in words.

   _____

   Using the same cards, what is the smallest two-digit number you can make?

   c) Write it in digits. _____

   d) Write it in words.

   _____

8. Circle the odd numbers.

Score:	Time taken:	Target met?

Target time: **12 minutes**

1. Solve these calculations.

   a) _____ + 13 = 20

   b) 31 + _____ = 38

   c) _____ + 5 = 35

2. Ravi writes down everything he spends his pocket money on. He has spent 80p this week.

   Sweets 10p
   Toy 20p
   Magazine ?

   How much was the magazine? _____

3. Emma has twenty-two teddy bears on her bed and another fifteen on her shelf.

   a) How many teddy bears does Emma have? _____

   b) She gets 3 more for her birthday. How many does she have now? _____

4. Lucy goes to a charity shop. She has 48p. She wants to buy a T-shirt for 80p.

   80p

   How much more money does she need? _____p

5. Solve these calculations.

   a) _____ + 6 = 37

   b) 47 − _____ = 42

6. There were 38 horses in a field. Sixteen ran away. How many horses were left? _____

7. Andy has a piece of hosepipe 100cm long. He cuts off 60cm. How much does he have left? _____cm

8. Solve these calculations.

   a) If 29 + 47 = 76, then 47 + 29 =
   _____

   b) If 58 + 28 = 86, then 86 − 58 =
   _____

9. Write **<**, **>** or **=** to make these statements correct.

   a) 7 + 2 _____ 3 + 4

   b) 9 − 3 _____ 6 − 1

   c) 10 − 4 _____ 3 + 3

10. Mark ✓ for a true statement and ✗ for a false statement.

    a) 30 + 40 = 70 _____

    b) 39 − 7 = 33 _____

    c) 27 − 20 = 17 _____

11. Solve the number riddle.

    I think of a number. Then I subtract 5 and add 3. The answer is 8. What was my number?

    _____

Score:		Time taken:		Target met?	

1. Solve these calculations.

   a) 5 + 5 + 5 + 5 + 5 + 5 = _____

   b) 2 + 2 + 2 + 2 + 2 + 2 + 2 = _____

   c) 10 + 10 + 10 = _____

2. Oranges come in packs of 5.
   Annabel buys 5 packs.
   How many oranges does
   she have? _____

3. Solve these calculations.

   a) 2 × 5 = _____

   b) 7 × 10 = _____

   c) 35 ÷ 5 = _____

   d) 12 ÷ 2 = _____

4. Ashraf bought 2 toy planes for 20p each.

   How much did he spend? _____ p

5. How many 10p coins would
   you need to make 70p? _____

6. Milan shared 20 lollies between
   herself and her 4 friends.
   How many lollies did they
   each get? _____

7. Circle the number that equals 2 × 3.

   12   3   8   6   10

8. Circle the number that equals 50 ÷ 10.

   10   15   3   20   5

9. Mark ✓ for a true statement and
   ✗ for a false statement.

   a) 5 × 8 = 45 _____

   b) 60 ÷ 5 = 12 _____

10. What fraction of each shape is shaded?

    a)

    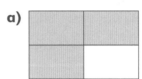

    _____

    b)

    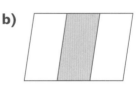

    _____

11. Circle $\frac{1}{3}$ of the mice.

12. Circle $\frac{3}{4}$ of the bananas.

    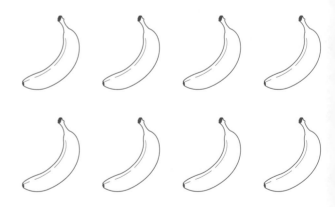

13. Jonah had 12 footballs.
    He kicked $\frac{1}{4}$ of them over
    the fence. How many did
    he kick over the fence? _____

Score:		Time taken:		Target met?	

Target time: **12 minutes**

1. Convert these measurements.

   a) 300cm = _____ m

   b) 400cm = _____ m

   c) 50cm = _____ m

   d) 6m = _____ cm

   e) 2000m = _____ km

   f) 6km = _____ m

2. Read these scales.

   a) How much does the drum weigh?

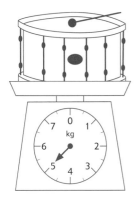

_____ kg

   b) How much do the books weigh?

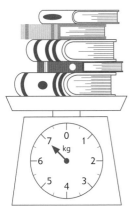

_____ kg

3. How many days are there
in 3 weeks?   _____

4. Hannah drinks half of her 240ml
of orange juice. How much is left? _____ ml

5. Raj's car can hold 60l of petrol.
If there is 20l left, how many
litres has Raj used?   _____ l

6. Daniel bought 3 magazines which cost
30p each.

   a) How much did Daniel spend?   _____ p

   b) What change would he
   have got from £1?   _____ p

   c) He was given 2 identical coins
   as his change. Which coins
   were they?   _____

   d) Does Daniel have enough
   money to buy another
   magazine?   _____

7. Look at this clock.

   a) What time is it?   _____

   b) What time will it
   be in 1 hour?   _____

8. Louie spends 20 minutes cleaning his
room, 10 minutes washing the dishes,
and 15 minutes washing the family car.

   a) How long does Louie spend
   doing his chores?   _____ min

   b) He gets pocket money every
   time he works for 1 hour.
   How much longer does he
   need to work to get his
   pocket money?   _____ min

9. Elin ran 100m in the school
Sports Day. She then ran
another 50m. How far did
she run?   _____ m

Score: _____   Time taken: _____   Target met? _____

1. The following pirate's map shows the location of some hidden treasure. X marks the spot!

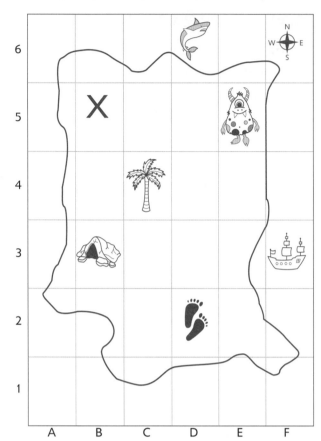

a) What can be found in square D2?

_____

b) Where is the palm tree? _____

c) In what position is the pirate ship? _____

d) If you travelled east from the cave, what would you find?

_____

e) In which direction is the shark from the footprints? _____

f) Which is the only square without any land in it? _____

g) Where is the treasure? _____

2. What is the proper 3D shape name for a ball?

_____

3. How many triangles can you see?

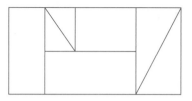

_____

4. Here is a cube.

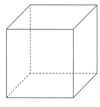

a) How many faces are there? _____

b) What shape are the faces? _____

c) Name another shape that has the same number of faces.

_____

d) How many edges does the cube have? _____

5. Draw the lines of symmetry on these letters.

6. If I am facing north and I make a half turn clockwise, which direction will I be facing? _____

7. If I am facing south and I make a quarter turn clockwise, which direction will I be facing? _____

Score:	Time taken:	Target met?

Notes for parents, tutors, teachers and other adult helpers

- **Maths Rapid Tests 1** is designed for six- and seven-year-olds, but may also be suitable for some older children.

- Remove this pull-out section before giving the book to the child.

- Before the child begins work on the first test, together read the instructions headed **What to do** on page 2. As you do so, point out to the child the suggested **Target time** for completing the test.

- Make sure the child has all the equipment in the list headed **What you need** on page 2. Also ensure that they are able to see a clock or a watch.

- There are three sections in this book. Each section consists of 12 tests. The first six tests focus on specific subject areas and the second six tests are a mix of these subject areas. Each mixed test will include questions from at least three of the subject areas. Details of the subject areas are given in the **Contents** page on page 3.

- Be sure that the child knows to tell you clearly when he or she has finished the test.

- When the child is ready, say 'Start the test now' and make a note of the start time.

- When the child has finished, make a note of the end time and then work out how long he or she took to complete the test. Then fill in the **Time taken** box, which appears at the end of the test.

- Mark the child's work using this pull-out section. Each test is out of 20 marks and each individual question is worth one mark – this means that if a question is split into parts, each part will be worth one mark unless otherwise stated in the answers. The unit of measure (for example, mm, cm, m, km, g and kg) does not need to be included as part of the answer to qualify for the mark. Then complete the **Score** box at the end of the test.

- This table shows you how to mark the **Target met?** box and the **Action** notes help you to plan the next step. However, these are suggestions only. Please use your own judgement as you decide how best to proceed.

Score	Time taken	Target met?	Action
1–9	Any	Not yet	Provide help and support as needed.
10–13	Any	Not yet	Encourage the child to keep practising using the tests in this book. The child may need to repeat some tests. If so, wait a few weeks or the child may simply remember the correct answers. Provide help and support as needed.
14–20	Over target – child took too long	Not yet	
14–20	On target – child took suggested time or less	Yes	Encourage the child to keep practising using further tests in this book, and to move on to the next book when you think this is appropriate.

- After finishing each test, the child should fill in the **Progress chart** on page 40.

- Whatever the test score, always encourage the child to have another go at the questions that he or she got wrong – without looking at the answers. If the child's answers are still incorrect, work through these questions together. Demonstrate the correct method if necessary.

- If the child struggles with particular question types or mathematical areas, help him or her to develop the skills and strategies needed.

Answers

Section 1 Test 1 (page 4)

1. **a)** 8, 10 (+ 2)
    b) 12, 15 (+ 3)

2. **a)** 8
    b) 20

3. 5   12   18   22   34

4. **a)** <
    b) <

5. **a)** twenty-seven
    b) thirty-eight

6. **a)** 13
    b) 28

7. **a)** 6
    b) 60
    c) 60

8. 27

9. 24, 52, 66

10. **a)** 3 or 4
    b) 8 or 9
    c) 1 or 2
    d) 6 or 7

Section 1 Test 2 (page 5)

1. 7

2. **a)** 4
    b) 5
    c) 7

3. **a)** 8
    b) 1
    c) 2

4. 7

5. 16 (11 + 5)

6. 17 min (13 min + 4 min)

7. **a)** 7
    b) 6

8. 19 (12 + 7)

9. 18 min (10 min + 8 min)

10. **a)** 31 + 27 = 58   } (can be either
    b) 27 + 31 = 58   } way round)
    c) 58 − 27 = 31

11. **a)** 4
    b) 8
    c) 13

Section 1 Test 3 (page 6)

1. **a)** 6, 8, 10
    b) 22, 24, 26

2. 6

3. 20

4. 30

5. 60 (10 × 6)

6. 6 (12 ÷ 2)

7. **a)** 6
    b) 40
    c) 40

8. 3 (15 ÷ 5)

9. 4 (8 ÷ 2)

10. **a)** 10 ÷ 2
    b) 14 ÷ 2
    c) 20 ÷ 5
    d) 15 ÷ 5

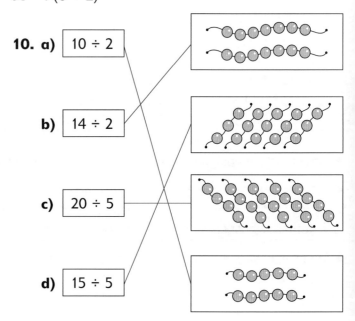

Schofield & Sims

11. a) any 1 rectangle shaded
b) any 1 square shaded
c) any 1 rectangle shaded
d) any 3 triangles shaded

Section 1 Test 4 (page 7)

1. a) 2cm
b) 3cm
c) 5cm
d) 4cm

2. 9cm (18cm ÷ 2)

3. a)

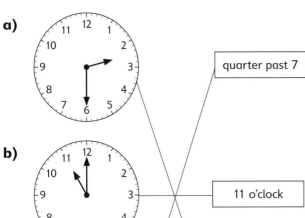

b)

c)

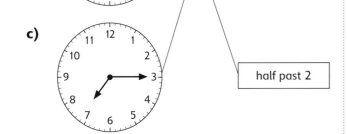

4. a) =
b) <
c) >

5. a) 56p
b) 52p
c) 87p
d) £1.76

6. a) 1kg
b) 3kg
c) 2000g

7. a) 300ml
b) 600ml

Section 1 Test 5 (page 8)

1.

2. a)

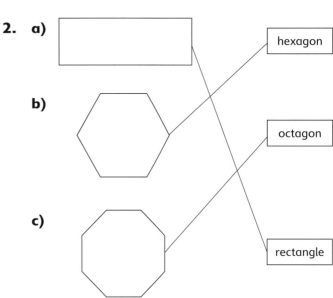

hexagon

b)

octagon

c)

rectangle

3. (1 mark for each correct row. Max. 4 marks.)

Shape	Number of sides	Number of corners
Square	4	4
Triangle	3	3
Pentagon	5	5
Hexagon	6	6

4. a) 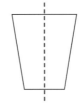   **b)**

c) 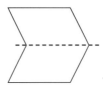   **d)**

Section 1 Test 5 (page 8) continued

5. (the only shape with 3 sides)

6. a)

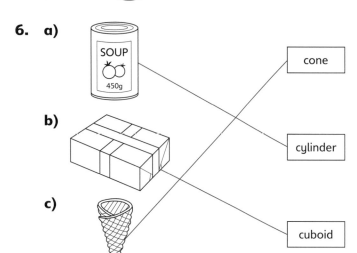

b)

c)

7. a) cylinder
   b) D3
   c) C1
   d) cube

Section 1 Test 6 (page 9)

1. (1 mark for each correct number. Max. 5 marks.)

Odd numbers	Even numbers
7 21	4 16 28

2. a) 4
   b) rabbit and hamster
   c) 4
   d) 25

3. a) (1 mark for each correct row. Max. 7 marks.)

Car colour	Tally	Total
White	ЖЖ IIII	9
Red	ЖЖ	5
Black	ЖЖ ЖЖ I	11
Silver	ЖЖ II	7
Grey	ЖЖ I	6
Yellow	II	2
Pink	I	1

   b) black
   c) pink
   d) 9
   e) silver

Section 1 Test 7 (page 10)

1. a) 20, 25 (+ 5)
   b) 44, 54 (+ 10)

2. a) 70
   b) 40

3. 60 min

4. 24 hr

5. (1 mark for each correct row. Max. 5 marks.)

Sport	Tally	Total
Football	ЖЖ ЖЖ ЖЖ ЖЖ II	22
Netball	ЖЖ ЖЖ ЖЖ II	17
Tennis	ЖЖ ЖЖ I	11
Rounders	ЖЖ ЖЖ ЖЖ ЖЖ ЖЖ I	26
Rugby	ЖЖ ЖЖ ЖЖ	15

Schofield & Sims

6. a) 71

b) 66

7. 200ml (400ml ÷ 2)

8. a) 2kg

b) 1kg

9. any 2 toy cars circled (8 ÷ 4)

10. (1 mark for a correct line of symmetry in either direction. Max. 1 mark.)

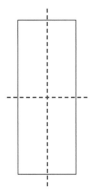

11. (check that the position of the hour hand is as shown below)

a)  **b)**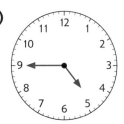

Section 1 Test 8 (page 11)

1. a) 51

b) 88

2. a) 9 (18 ÷ 2)

b) 5 (20 ÷ 4)

3. 4p (20p − 16p)

4. 150ml (100ml + 50ml)

5. (1 mark for each correct reflection. Max. 4 marks.)

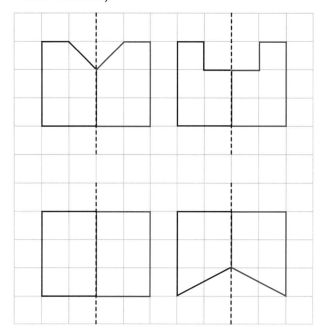

6. a) 21 (14 + 7)

b) 7 (the overlapping area shows those who are 9 and also have black hair)

c) 9 (any number outside the '9 years old' circle)

7. 6 (60 ÷ 10)

8. a) 1m

b) 50cm

c) 200cm

d) 400cm

9. a) 200cm (100cm × 2)

b) 50cm (100cm ÷ 2)

Section 1 Test 9 (page 12)

1. 39 26 22 8 0

2. 11 15 28 34 56

3. any 5 sweets circled (10 ÷ 2)

4. a) 28

b) 75

c) 13

d) 6

5. a) $\frac{1}{4}$

b) $\frac{1}{2}$

Answers

Section 1 Test 9 (page 12) continued

6. **a)** 10
   b) 40
7. **a)** 90g (45g × 2)
   b) 180g (90g × 2)
8. **a)** 5cm
   b) 3cm
9. **a)** 600ml
   b) 800ml
10. 7p (20p − 13p)
11. 7 (7 × 2 = 14)
12. 10 (10 + 12 = 22)

Section 1 Test 10 (page 13)

1. **a)** 8
   b) 100
2. **a)** ✗
   b) ✓
   c) ✓
   d) ✗
   e) ✓
3. **a)** 1kg
   b) 3kg
4. **a)** 50p (20p + 30p)
   b) 50p (£1 − 50p)
5. **a)** 2 (8 ÷ 4)
   b) 2 (6 ÷ 3)
6. **a)** 1 or 2
   b) 8 or 9
   c) 45 to 55 (accept any number between 45 and 55)
   d) 78 to 88 (accept any number between 78 and 88)
7. triangular prism
8. **a)** 14 (remember that each image is worth 2 children)
   b) 6

Section 1 Test 11 (page 14)

1. 45p (5 × 9p)
2. any 3 flowers circled (6 ÷ 2)
3. **a)** 3cm
   b) 4cm
4. **a)** 2l
   b) 3000ml
   c) 5000ml
5. 2
6. **a)** 8 (15 − 7)
   b) 4 (8 − 4)
7. **a)** 11 (18 − 7)
   b) 9 (11 − 2)
8. **a)** 75
   b) seventy-five
   c) 57
   d) fifty-seven
9. **a)** 20 (all numbers in the 'Chocolate pudding' circle)
   b) 7 (number in the overlap)
   c) 9 (number outside the circles)
10. 42kg (21kg × 2)

Section 1 Test 12 (page 15)

1. **a)** $\frac{1}{3}$
   b) $\frac{1}{2}$ or $\frac{2}{4}$
2. 95 68 57 37 21
3. 38 46 59 70 100
4. 36 (12 × 2 = 24, 24 + 12 = 36)
5. **a)** 7
   b) 4
   c) 49
   d) 60
   e) 70
6. the number 16 circled

Schofield & Sims

7. the number 7 circled

8. **a)** 7

   b) broccoli and onions

   c) 1

   d) 18 (all the bars added together)

9. **a)**

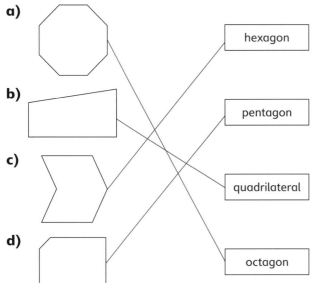

   b)

   c)

   d)

Section 2 Test 1 (page 16)

1. **a)** 20

   b) 7

   c) 70

2. **a)** forty-nine

   b) eighty-three

3. **a)** 476

   b) 664

   c) 368

   d) 347

4. 46, 48, 50

5. **a)** >

   b) <

   c) <

6. **a)** 120

   b) 82

7. **a)** 98

   b) ninety-eight

   c) 89

   d) eighty-nine

8. 7, 15, 23

Section 2 Test 2 (page 17)

1. **a)** 7

   b) 7

   c) 30

2. 50p (10p + 20p = 30p, 80p − 30p = 50p)

3. **a)** 37 (22 + 15)

   b) 40 (37 + 3)

4. 32p (80p − 48p)

5. **a)** 31

   b) 5

6. 22 (38 − 16)

7. 40cm (100cm − 60cm)

8. **a)** 76

   b) 28

9. **a)** >

   b) >

   c) =

10. **a)** ✓

   b) ✗

   c) ✗

11. 10 (work backwards: 8 − 3 = 5, 5 + 5 = 10)

Section 2 Test 3 (page 18)

1. **a)** 30

   b) 14

   c) 30

2. 25 (5 × 5)

3. **a)** 10

   b) 70

   c) 7

   d) 6

Answers

Section 2 Test 3 (page 18) continued

4. 40p (20p × 2)

5. 7 (70 ÷ 10)

6. 4 (She and her 4 friends make 5 people. 20 ÷ 5.)

7. the number 6 circled

8. the number 5 circled

9. **a)** ✗
   b) ✓

10. **a)** $\frac{3}{4}$
    b) $\frac{1}{3}$

11. any 2 mice circled (6 ÷ 3)

12. any 6 bananas circled (8 ÷ 4 = 2, 2 × 3 = 6)

13. 3 (12 ÷ 4)

Section 2 Test 4 (page 19)

1. **a)** 3m
   b) 4m
   c) $\frac{1}{2}$m
   d) 600cm
   e) 2km
   f) 6000m

2. **a)** 5kg
   b) 7kg

3. 21 (3 × 7)

4. 120ml (240ml ÷ 2)

5. 40l (60l − 20l)

6. **a)** 90p (3 × 30p)
   b) 10p (£1 − 90p)
   c) 5 pence coins
   d) no (he only has 10p and needs 30p)

7. **a)** 4 o'clock
   b) 5 o'clock

8. **a)** 45 min (20 min + 10 min + 15 min)
   b) 15 min (60 min − 45 min)

9. 150m (100m + 50m)

Section 2 Test 5 (page 20)

1. **a)** footprints
   b) C4
   c) F3
   d) pirate ship
   e) north
   f) A1
   g) B5

2. sphere

3. 4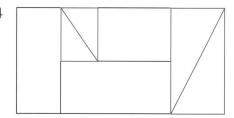

4. **a)** 6
   b) square
   c) cuboid or pentagonal-based pyramid
   d) 12

5. (1 mark for each correct line. Max. 5 marks.)

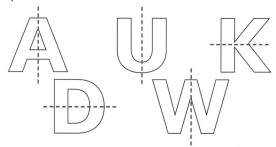

6. south

7. west

Section 2 Test 6 (page 21)

1. **a)** 21 (all numbers in the 'Science' circle)
   b) 4 (number in the overlap)
   c) 8 (number outside the circles)
   d) 41 (add all numbers)

2. **a)** 12 (remember that each image is worth 2 children)
   b) 4
   c) footballer
   d) 34

3. (1 mark for each correct section.
Max. 4 marks.)

	Less than 40	Greater than 40
Odd	7	67 71 49
Even	34 12	98 54

4. **a)** (1 mark for each correct bar. Max. 5 marks.)

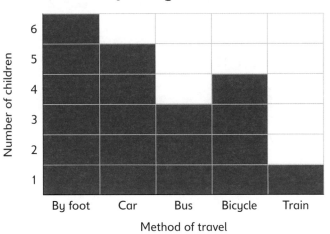

b) 13 (car, bus, bicycle and train all have wheels)

c) 5

d) 19 (add all results together)

Section 2 Test 7 (page 22)

1. **a)** Daisy

b) Bella

c) Emma

d) Alia

e) Claire

2. 200ml (400ml ÷ 2)

3. **a)** 7kg

b) 4000g

c) 400cm

d) 2l

4. 19 (8 + 7 + 4)

5. 24 (16 + 5 + 3)

6. 7   13   18   27   41

7. **a)** 10 (remember that each image is worth 2 children)

b) 12

c) 17 (32 children altogether, 32 − 15)

8. (1 mark for each correct reflection. Max. 4 marks.)

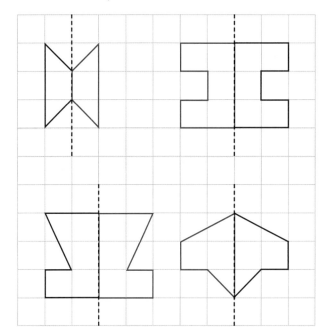

Section 2 Test 8 (page 23)

1. **a)** 2 to 4 (accept any number between 2 and 4)

b) 12 to 14 (accept any number between 12 and 14)

2. **a)** fifty-two

b) seventy-four

3. **a)** 85

b) 24

4. **a)** 69

b) 54

c) 37

d) 41

e) 21

5. 15 (30 ÷ 2)

Answers

Section 2 Test 8 (page 23) continued

6. 8

7. cylinder

8. 24 (48 ÷ 2)

9. 9 (36 ÷ 4)

10. any 6 cats circled (12 ÷ 2)

11. any 4 tennis balls circled (16 ÷ 4)

12. a) 440g (220g × 2)
   b) 110g (220g ÷ 2)

Section 2 Test 9 (page 24)

1. a) 25 (all numbers in the 'Gymnastics' circle)
   b) 4 (number in the overlap)
   c) 12 (There were 19 in craft club. 19 − 7.)
   d) 14 (number outside the circles)

2. a) 11
   b) 16
   c) 25
   d) 24

3. a) 8 (80 ÷ 10)
   b) 40 (80 ÷ 2)

4. 30cm (5cm × 6)

5. a) 3cm
   b) 5cm
   c) 2cm
   d) 4cm

6. a) 75p (50p + 25p)
   b) 10p (40p + 50p = 90p, £1 − 90p = 10p)
   c) duck and bear (35p + 50p = 85p)

7. 700 (100 × 7 or 100 added 7 times)

8. 3 o'clock

Section 2 Test 10 (page 25)

1. a) 8 (16 ÷ 4 = 4, 4 × 2 = 8)
   b) 10 (20 ÷ 2)
   c) 3 (12 ÷ 4)
   d) 12 (16 ÷ 4 = 4, 4 × 3 = 12)

2. a) 20ml
   b) 80ml
   c) 600ml
   d) 9l

3. 30 (150 − 120)

4. 6 (work backwards: 16 − 4 = 12, 12 ÷ 2 = 6)

5. 20 (40 ÷ 2)

6. a) 24 (8 + 16)
   b) 20 (8 + 12)
   c) 41 (8 + 16 + 12 + 5)

7. half past 10 or 10:30

8. 60

9. a) 3
   b) 9
   c) 8

10. $\frac{1}{2}$ or $\frac{2}{4}$

Section 2 Test 11 (page 26)

1. cube

2. square-based pyramid

3. a) £1.37
   b) 23p (£1.60 − £1.37)
   c) £1.57 (£1.37 + 20p)

4. a) 1mm   30cm   1m $2\frac{1}{2}$m   5km
   b) 1g   300g $\frac{1}{2}$kg   1000g   2kg

5. 90 (9 × 10)

6. 3, 4 (3 + 4 = 7, 3 × 4 = 12)

7. **a)** 10

   b) 48

   c) 5

   d) 15

   e) (1 mark for each correct bar. Max. 7 marks.)

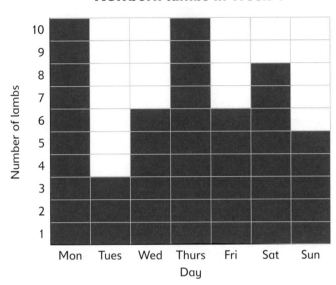

Newborn lambs in Week 1

Section 2 Test 12 (page 27)

1. 3kg

2. **a)** 6

   b) 41

   c) 26

   d) 42

   e) 25

3. **a)** $\frac{3}{4}$

   b) $\frac{1}{2}$ or $\frac{2}{4}$

4. (1 mark for each correct shape circled. Max. 2 marks. Hexagons have 6 sides.)

5. 180m (100m + 50m + 30m)

6. **a)**

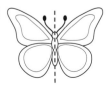

   b)

7. **a)**

(check that the position of the hour hand is as shown)

   b)

(check that the position of the hour hand is as shown)

8. **a)** north

   b) west

9. **a)** 35 (12 + 10 + 13)

   b) 70 (35 × 2)

   c) 18 (13 + 5)

Section 3 Test 1 (page 28)

1. **a)** 70

   b) 7

   c) 7

   d) 70

2. (numbers in rows add 1 and numbers in columns add 10)

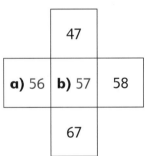

	47	
a) 56	b) 57	58
	67	

	c) 62	
71	72	d) 73
	82	

3. **a)** 57, 67 (+ 10)

   b) 49, 39 (− 10)

   c) 35, 25 (− 10)

4. **a)** <

   b) >

5. **a)** 18   27   45   54   72

   b) 49   58   62   109   121

Answers

Section 3 Test 1 (page 28) continued

6. a) 731
   b) 137

7. a) 90
   b) 3
   c) 0

Section 3 Test 2 (page 29)

1. a) 35
   b) 63
   c) 42
   d) 50

2. a) >
   b) =
   c) =
   d) <

3. 44 (25 + 6 + 13)

4. 22 (26 − 13 = 13, 13 + 9 = 22)

5. a) 80
   b) 40
   c) 65
   d) 45

6. 45 (10 + 15 + 20)

7. 16 (24 + 12 = 36, 52 − 36 = 16)

8. 14°C (21°C − 7°C)

9. 71 (46 + 21 + 4)

10. 23 (37 − 14)

11. 40p (85p − 45p)

Section 3 Test 3 (page 30)

1. a) 12
   b) 42

2. 30 (6 × 5)

3. 80 (8 × 10)

4. a) 8
   b) 12

5. a) $5 \times 9 = 45$ } (can be either
   b) $9 \times 5 = 45$ } way round)
   c) $45 \div 9 = 5$ } (can be either
   d) $45 \div 5 = 9$ } way round)

6. 10 (15 ÷ 3 = 5 so 5 were eaten. 15 − 5 = 10 were left.)

7. a) 11 (22 ÷ 2)
   b) 4 (12 ÷ 3)
   c) 9 ($\frac{2}{4}$ is the same as $\frac{1}{2}$. 18 ÷ 2 = 9)
   d) 15 (20 ÷ 4 = 5, 5 × 3 = 15)

8. any 2 small rectangles shaded (6 ÷ 3)

9. any 6 sections shaded (8 ÷ 4 = 2, 2 × 3 = 6)

10. a) any 2 squares shaded ($\frac{1}{2} = \frac{2}{4}$)
    b) 2 (To find an equivalent fraction, the numerator [top number] and denominator [bottom number] must be multipled or divided by the same number. Here, both denominators are given but the numerator is missing in the second fraction. To find the missing number, do to the numerators what has been done to the denominators. So 2 × 2 = 4, 1 × 2 = 2.)

11. 6 (24 ÷ 4)

Section 3 Test 4 (page 31)

1. a) 500g
   b) 1500g
   c) 4500g
   d) 25cm
   e) 150cm

2. a) ten past four
   b) twenty to eleven
   c) twenty-five past seven
   d) five to six

3. a) 45 min (15 min × 3)
   b) 4km (1 hr = 60 min, 60 ÷ 15 = 4)

4. 7kg (3.5kg × 2 or 3.5kg + 3.5kg)

5. a) 74p (43p + 31p)
   b) 83p (26p + 26p + 31p)

c) 5p (15p + 15p + 15p = 45p,
50p − 45p = 5p)

6. a) 7°C

b) 4°C

c) 9°C

7. a) 300ml (600ml ÷ 2)

b) 250ml (500ml ÷ 2)

Section 3 Test 5 (page 32)

1. (1 mark for each correct line. Max. 10 marks.)

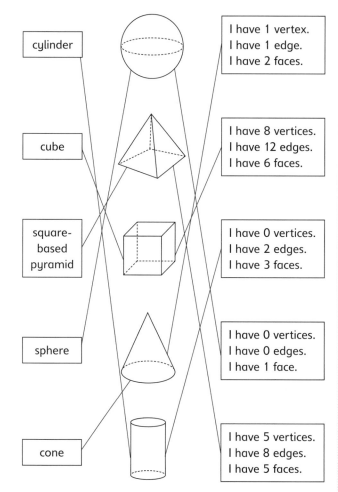

2. a) triangle ⎱ (can be either
b) square ⎰ way round)
c) circle ⎱ (can be either
d) rectangle ⎰ way round)
e) triangle ⎱ (can be either
f) rectangle ⎰ way round)

3. a) (a quarter turn is a quarter of a full-circle turn)

b) (3 quarter turns)

c) (half of a full-circle turn)

4. B

Section 3 Test 6 (page 33)

1. a) (1 mark for each correct row. Max. 5 marks. Remember that each image is worth 2 lollies.)

Lemon	
Banana	
Lime	
Cola	
Grape	

b) lemon

c) grape

d) cola and grape (5 + 3 = 8)

e) 30 (8 + 12 + 10)

f) 12 (38 were sold in total. 50 − 38 = 12.)

2. (1 mark for each correct shape. Max. 4 marks.)

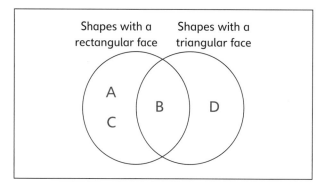

Answers

Section 3 Test 6 (page 33) continued

3. (1 mark for each correct row. Max. 6 marks.)

Fruit	Tally	Total
Apple	卌 ||	7
Orange	卌 |	6
Pear	卌	5
Cherry	卌	5
Nectarine	卌	5
Strawberry	卌 |	6

Section 3 Test 7 (page 34)

1. 17 (47 − 30)

2. **a)** 28p (14p × 2)
b) 2p (30p − 28p)

3. **a)** $\frac{1}{2}$
b) $\frac{3}{4}$
c) $1\frac{1}{4}$
d) $2\frac{1}{2}$

4. **a)** 25p (50p ÷ 2)
b) 42p (84p ÷ 2)
c) 24p (48p ÷ 2)
d) 18p (36p ÷ 2)

5. **a)** 49
b) 24
c) 60
d) 8

6. **a)** 400g
b) 700g

7. **a)** 3
b) 8 and 12
c) 17 (bigger than size 10 means 11 and 12 – it does not include size 10)

Section 3 Test 8 (page 35)

1. (1 mark for each. Max. 2 marks. Quadrilaterals have 4 sides.)

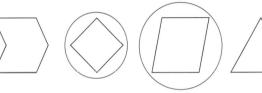

2. **a)** 5:15
b) 8:05

3. 20km (He walks 4km a day over 5 school days. 4km × 5 = 20km.)

4. **a)** 250ml
b) 550ml

5. **a)** 3l
b) 500ml
c) 4000ml
d) $2\frac{1}{2}$l

6. **a)** any 3 sections shaded (4 ÷ 4 = 1, 1 × 3 = 3)
b) any 6 triangles shaded (8 ÷ 4 = 2, 2 × 3 = 6)

7. 5 (15 ÷ 3)

8. 9 (12 ÷ 4 = 3 so he gives 3 away. 12 − 3 = 9.)

9. **a)** (a right-angled turn is a quarter turn)

b)

10. **a)** =
b) >
c) <

Schofield & Sims

Section 3 Test 9 (page 36)

1. **a)** 9°C
   b) 14°C
   c) 9°C

2. 60m (25m + 20m + 15m)

3. 3 (work backwards: 14 ÷ 2 = 7, 7 − 4 = 3)

4. 12 (work backwards: 19 − 12 = 7, 7 + 5 = 12)

5. (1 mark for each correct section. Max. 4 marks.)

	Multiples of 5	Not multiples of 5
Multiples of 2	20 30	32 16
Not multiples of 2	15 55	11 37

6. 78 (56 + 22)

7. **a)** 7:05
   b) 7:25
   c) 4:35
   d) 4:55

8. **a)** 6 o'clock or 6:00
   b) half past six or 6:30

9. **a)** 210kg (420kg ÷ 2)
   b) 420kg (840kg ÷ 2)

10. £2 (£1.50 + £1.50 = £3, £5 − £3 = £2)

Section 3 Test 10 (page 37)

1. **a)** 700ml
   b) 450ml

2. **a)** 50cm (100cm ÷ 2)
   b) 25cm (50cm ÷ 2)

3. **a)** 28
   b) 44

4. (1 mark for each answer. Max. 8 marks.)

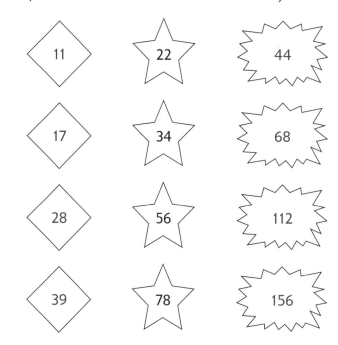

5. (check that the position of the hour hand is as shown below)

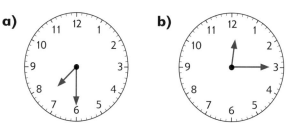

6. **a)** black
   b) Siamese
   c) 18
   d) 58 (add up all the bars)

Section 3 Test 11 (page 38)

1. **a)** 60
   b) 30
   c) 78
   d) 4

2. **a)** $\frac{2}{6}$ or $\frac{1}{3}$
   b) $\frac{4}{8}$ or $\frac{1}{2}$

3. any 12 fish circled (16 ÷ 4 = 4, 4 × 3 = 12)

Answers

Section 3 Test 11 (page 38) continued

4. 36 (38 − 10 = 28, 28 + 8 = 36)

5. **a)** $3\frac{1}{2}$ cm

    b) $4\frac{1}{2}$ cm

6. **a)** (1 mark for each correct answer. Max. 4 marks.)

    I have 5 faces.

    I have 9 edges.

    I have 6 vertices.

    I am a triangular prism.

    b) (1 mark for each correct answer. Max. 4 marks.)

    I have 6 faces.

    I have 12 edges.

    I have 8 vertices.

    I am a cuboid.

7. 32 (partitioning: add 10 × 2 to 6 × 2 = 32)

8. 30 (6 × 5)

Section 3 Test 12 (page 39)

1. **a)** 18, 21 (+ 3)

    b) 14, 9 (− 5)

    c) 106, 116 (+ 10)

2. **a)** 90p (45p + 45p)

    b) 70p (45p + 25p)

    c) lolly and car (25p + 30p = 55p)

    d) 5p (60p − 55p)

    e) 10p (30p + 60p = 90p, £1 − 90p = 10p)

3. **a)** 6cm (24cm ÷ 4)

    b) 17cm ($\frac{2}{4} = \frac{1}{2}$, 34cm ÷ 2)

    c) 2cm (6cm ÷ 3)

    d) 6cm (8cm ÷ 4 = 2cm, 2cm × 3 = 6cm)

4. 32 (14 + 12 + 6)

5. 11 (55 ÷ 5. Children can work this out by counting in 5s.)

6. **a)** 150g

    b) 950g

7. **a)** star

    b) B5

    c) sun

    d) D4

This book of answers is a pull-out section from **Maths Rapid Tests 1**.

Published by **Schofield & Sims Ltd**,
7 Mariner Court, Wakefield, West Yorkshire WF4 3FL, UK
Telephone 01484 607080
www.schofieldandsims.co.uk

This edition copyright © Schofield & Sims Ltd, 2018
First published in 2018

Author: **Rebecca Brant**. Rebecca Brant has asserted her moral rights under the Copyright, Designs and Patents Act, 1988, to be identified as the author of this work.

British Library Cataloguing in Publication Data. A catalogue record for this book is available from the British Library.

Design by **Ledgard Jepson Ltd**
Printed in the UK by **Page Bros (Norwich) Ltd**

ISBN 978 07217 1421 9

Statistics

Target time: **12 minutes**

1. The Venn diagram shows the favourite school subjects of a group of children.

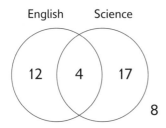

English   Science

12   4   17

8

a) How many children like science? _____

b) How many children like both English and science? _____

c) How many children do not like either English or science? _____

d) How many children were surveyed? _____

2. The pictogram below shows the dream jobs of children in class 2R.

♡ = 2 children

Footballer	♡ ♡ ♡ ♡ ♡
Astronaut	♡
Singer	♡ ♡
Teacher	♡ ♡ ♡ ♡ ♡ ♡
Doctor	♡ ♡ ♡

a) How many children want to be a teacher? _____

b) How many more children want to be a doctor than an astronaut? _____

c) What is the second most popular job?

_____

d) How many children are in the class? _____

3. Write each of these numbers in the correct part of the Carroll diagram.

7, 34, 67, 12, 71, 49, 98, 54

	Less than 40	Greater than 40
Odd		
Even		

4. a) Use the following information about how children travel to school to complete the block diagram.

Method of travel	Number of children
By foot	6
Car	5
Bus	3
Bicycle	4
Train	1

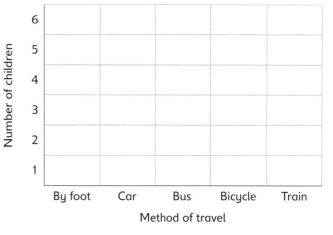

Journeys to school

b) How many children needed wheels to get to school? _____

c) How many more children walked than got the train? _____

d) How many children took part in the survey? _____

| Score: | | Time taken: | | Target met? | |

Maths Rapid Tests 1

Target time: **12 minutes**

1. A group of friends ran a race. Emma beat Alia. Daisy came first. Bella finished right behind Daisy. Claire finished last. Write each girl's name next to the correct position.

   a) 1st _____

   b) 2nd _____

   c) 3rd _____

   d) 4th _____

   e) 5th _____

2. There is 400ml of liquid in Bottle A. There is half as much in Bottle B. How much liquid is in Bottle B? _____ml

3. Convert these measurements.

   a) 7000g = _____ kg

   b) 4kg = _____ g

   c) 4m = _____ cm

   d) 2000ml = _____ l

4. Maisie went to the library to borrow some books. She borrowed 8 fiction books and 7 non-fiction books. She then went to the shops and bought 4 more books. How many books did Maisie have? _____

5. Nadiya received 16 presents at her birthday party. Her mum gave her 5 more and her aunty gave her another 3. How many presents did she receive altogether? _____

6. Write these numbers in order, smallest first.

   41   13   27   7   18

   _____

7. The pictogram shows the favourite colours of children in a Year 2 class.

✱ = 2 children

Blue	✱ ✱ ✱ ✱ ✱
Yellow	✱
Red	✱ ✱ ✱
Orange	✱ ✱
Pink	✱
Green	✱ ✱ ✱ ✱

   a) How many children preferred the most popular colour? _____

   b) How many children liked red, orange or pink? _____

   c) If 15 boys took part in the survey, how many girls were asked? _____

8. Use a ruler to complete these symmetrical shapes.

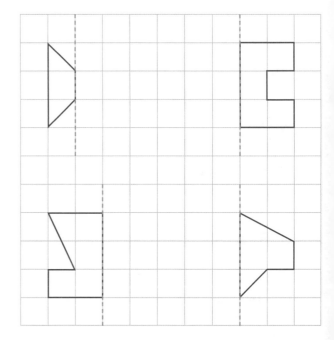

Target time: **12 minutes**

1. Estimate these numbers on the number line.

a) _____   b) _____

2. Write these numbers in words.

a) 52   _____

b) 74   _____

3. Write these numbers in digits.

a) Eighty-five   _____

b) Twenty-four   _____

4. Solve these calculations.

a) 62 + 7 =   _____

b) 34 + 20 =   _____

c) What is 27 add 10?   _____

d) What is 2 less than 43? _____

e) What is 27 subtract 6? _____

5. Danny shared 30 chocolate
buttons between 2 bowls.
How many buttons were
in each bowl?   _____

6. How many sides does an
octagon have?   _____

7. I have 1 curved face and 2 flat circular faces.
Which 3D shape am I?

_____

8. John had 48 dinosaurs. He
gave $\frac{1}{2}$ away. How many
was he left with?   _____

9. Simran had 36 friendship bracelets.
She gave $\frac{1}{4}$ of them to her friends.
How many did she give away?   _____

10. Circle $\frac{1}{2}$ of the cats.

11. Circle $\frac{1}{4}$ of the tennis balls.

12. The pencil case weighs half as much as the
book and twice as much as the calculator.
How much do the other items weigh?

220g

a) _____g

b) _____g

Score: [   ]   Time taken: [   ]   Target met? [   ]

Target time: **12 minutes**

1. The Venn diagram shows after-school activities.

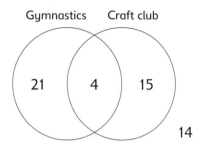

Gymnastics   Craft club

21   4   15

14

a) How many children went to gymnastics? _____

b) How many children went to both gymnastics and the craft club? _____

c) If 7 members of the craft club were girls, how many were boys? _____

d) How many children didn't go to either gymnastics or the craft club? _____

2. Solve these calculations.

a) 25 − 14 = _____

b) 29 − 13 = _____

c) 46 − 21 = _____

d) 58 − 34 = _____

3. Biscuits come in packets of 10.

a) Sarah needs 80 biscuits for a party. How many packets does she need to buy? _____

b) If everyone has 2 biscuits, how many people are at the party? _____

4. If an eraser was 5cm long, how long would 6 erasers end to end measure? _____ cm

5. Measure the length of these arrows to the nearest centimetre.

a) 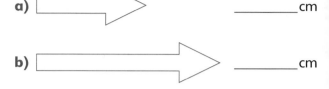 _____ cm

b)  _____ cm

c) _____ cm

d)  _____ cm

6. Ruby went shopping and found the following items.

50p   40p

35p   25p

a) How much would it cost her to buy the bear and the doll? _____ p

b) If she bought the kite and the bear, how much change would she get from £1? _____ p

c) Ruby spent 85p. What did she buy?

_____

7. Sammy was looking through some old photo albums. There were 7 albums and he counted 100 photos in each album. How many photos were there altogether? _____

8. The school day starts at 9 o'clock and lasts 6 hours. At what time does it end? _____

Score: _____   Time taken: _____   Target met? _____

Target time: **12 minutes**

1. Find these numbers.

a) What is $\frac{2}{4}$ of 16? _____

b) What is $\frac{1}{2}$ of 20? _____

c) What is $\frac{1}{4}$ of 12? _____

d) What is $\frac{3}{4}$ of 16? _____

2. How much liquid is in each container?

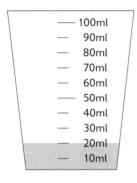

a) _____

b) _____

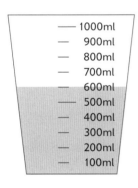

c) _____

d) _____

3. There were 150 seats on an aeroplane. There were only 120 passengers. How many empty seats were there? _____

4. Tia thinks of a number. She multiplies it by 2 then adds 4. The answer is 16. What was her number? _____

5. Fatima shared her 40 strawberry shoelaces between herself and her best friend. How many laces did they each get? _____

6. The Carroll diagram shows the number of children at an after-school club.

	Younger than 7	Older than 7
Boy	8	16
Girl	12	5

a) How many boys attended the club? _____

b) How many children under 7 were there at the club? _____

c) How many children in total were at the club? _____

7. Freddy went for a run with his dad at 10 o'clock. They ran for 30 minutes. At what time did they get home? _____

8. What is 12 × 5? _____

9. Solve these calculations.

a) 17 + _____ = 20

b) 10 + _____ = 19

c) 20 − _____ = 12

10. What fraction of this shape is shaded?

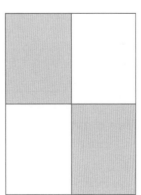

_____

Score: _____   Time taken: _____   Target met? _____

Target time: **12 minutes**

1. I have 6 square faces, 8 vertices and 12 edges. Which 3D shape am I?

   _____

2. I have 1 square face and 4 triangular faces. Which 3D shape am I?

   _____

3. This is Penny's purse.

   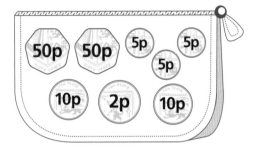

   a) How much money does Penny have?   £_____

   b) She thought she had £1.60. How much less does she actually have?   _____p

   c) She found a 20p coin in the sofa. How much money does she have now?   £_____

4. Write these measurements in order, smallest first.

   a) 1m   30cm $2\frac{1}{2}$m   1mm   5km

   _____

   b) 1g   2kg   300g $\frac{1}{2}$kg   1000g

   _____

5. Jim collected 9 badges. His friend Ralph collected 10 times as many. How many badges did Ralph have?   _____

6. Which pair of numbers has a sum of 7 and multiplies together to make 12? Circle the correct answer.

   1, 6   2, 5   3, 4

7. The tally chart below shows the number of lambs born over a three-week period.

Day	Week 1	Week 2	Week 3
Monday	𝍉𝍉	𝍉 ||	𝍉	
Tuesday	|||	𝍉 |||	||||
Wednesday	𝍉		𝍉 ||	|||
Thursday	𝍉𝍉	𝍉		𝍉
Friday	𝍉		𝍉 ||||	𝍉	
Saturday	𝍉 |||	𝍉		||||
Sunday	𝍉	𝍉 ||	|||

   a) How many lambs were born on the first Monday?   _____

   b) How many lambs were born in the first week?   _____

   c) How many more lambs were born on the second Tuesday than on the first?   _____

   d) How many lambs were born on Sundays over the 3 weeks?   _____

   e) Use the information from the tally chart to complete a block diagram to show the number of lambs born in Week 1.

   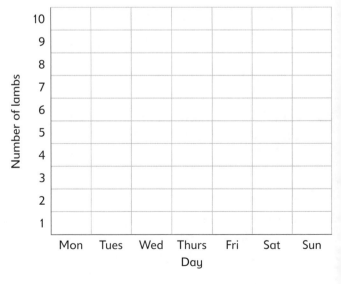

Newborn lambs in Week 1

1. How much does the bag weigh?

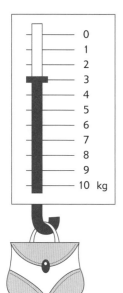

_____ kg

2. Solve these calculations.

a) 47 + _____ = 53

b) _____ + 23 = 64

c) 58 − _____ = 32

d) 64 − _____ = 22

e) 49 − _____ = 24

3. What fraction of each shape is shaded?

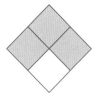

a) _____   b) _____

4. Circle the hexagons.

5. Sarah walked 100m, ran 50m and then walked a further 30m. How far did she travel?   _____ m

6. Draw the line of symmetry on each picture.

a)    b)

7. Draw the hands on the clocks so they show the correct time.

a) half past 1

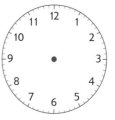

b) 7 o'clock

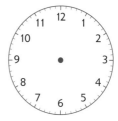

8. Look at this compass.

a) If I am facing east and I make a quarter turn anticlockwise, which direction will I be facing? _____

b) If I am facing north and I make a three-quarter turn clockwise, which direction will I be facing? _____

9. While bird-watching, Ella saw 12 blackbirds, 10 sparrows and 13 robins.

a) How many birds did she spot? _____

b) How many legs would that be altogether? _____

c) She then saw 5 more robins. How many robins did she spot altogether? _____

Score:		Time taken:		Target met?	

Target time: **12 minutes**

1. What is the value of the 7 digit in each of these numbers?

a) 74 _____

b) 107 _____

c) 87 _____

d) 173 _____

2. The following diagrams show parts of a hundred square. Write the missing numbers.

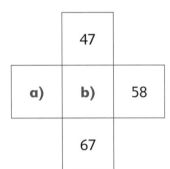

a) _____

b) _____

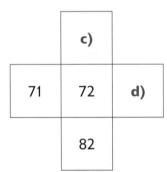

c) _____

d) _____

3. Complete these sequences.

a) 17, 27, 37, 47, _____, _____

b) 89, 79, 69, 59, _____, _____

c) 75, 65, 55, 45, _____, _____

4. Write **<** or **>** to make these statements correct.

a) 18 _____ 81

b) 54 _____ 38

5. Write these numbers in order, smallest first.

a)

_____

b)

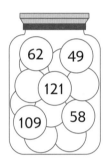

_____

6. Look at these number cards.

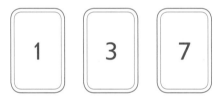

a) Using these cards, what is the largest three-digit number you can make? _____

b) Using the same cards, what is the smallest three-digit number you can make? _____

7. What is the value of each underlined digit?

a) 9̲5 _____

b) 15̲3 _____

c) 50̲7 _____

Target time: **12 minutes**

1. Solve these calculations.

a) 25 + 10 = _____

b) 43 + 20 = _____

c) 72 − 30 = _____

d) 65 − 15 = _____

2. Write **<**, **>** or **=** to make these statements correct.

a) 13 + 11 _____ 18 + 4

b) 21 − 5 _____ 8 + 8

c) 33 + 21 _____ 25 + 29

d) 41 − 22 _____ 38 − 17

3. Ethan was sent 25 birthday cards on his birthday. He received 6 more the following day and then got another 13 from some friends at school. How many birthday cards did he have? _____

4. Vicky has 26 stickers. She gives 13 away and then buys another 9. How many stickers does she have now? _____

5. Solve these calculations.

a) 20 + _____ = 100

b) _____ + 60 = 100

c) If 35 + 65 = 100, then 100 − 35 =

_____

d) If 45 + 55 = 100, then 100 − 55 =

_____

6. Ed ate 10 cashew nuts, 15 Brazil nuts and 20 peanuts. How many nuts did he eat altogether? _____

7. Cameron had a piñata at his birthday party.

Twenty-four sweets fell out of the piñata on his first hit. On his second hit, a further 12 fell out. If there were 52 sweets in the piñata to start with, how many were still left in there? _____

8. The temperature at midday was 21°C. By evening it had dropped by 7°C. What was the temperature in the evening?

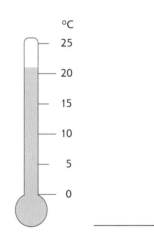

_____°C

9. Rachel had 46 fancy erasers. She found another 21 in a charity shop and her best friend Ella bought her 4 for her birthday. How many erasers does she have now? _____

10. Rajid had 37 bouncy balls. He gave 14 to his younger brother. How many did he keep? _____

11. Manny had 85p. He bought a bar of chocolate for 45p. How much money did he have left? _____p

Score: _____   Time taken: _____   Target met? _____

Target time: **12 minutes**

1. Solve these calculations.

   a) If $3 \times 4 = 12$, then $4 \times 3 =$ _____

   b) If $7 \times 6 = 42$, then $6 \times 7 =$ _____

2. How many fingers on 6 hands?

   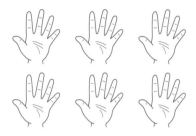

   _____

3. How many toes would 8 people have? _____

4. Solve these calculations.

   a) If $8 \times 2 = 16$, then $16 \div 2 =$ _____

   b) If $5 \times 12 = 60$, then $60 \div 5 =$ _____

5. Using only the following 3 numbers, write 4 calculations.

   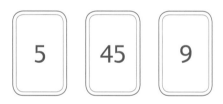

   a) _____ × _____ = _____

   b) _____ × _____ = _____

   c) _____ ÷ _____ = _____

   d) _____ ÷ _____ = _____

6. Gerry made 15 cupcakes. If $\frac{1}{3}$ were eaten, how many were left?

   _____

7. Find these numbers.

   a) What is $\frac{1}{2}$ of 22? _____

   b) What is $\frac{1}{3}$ of 12? _____

   c) What is $\frac{2}{4}$ of 18? _____

   d) What is $\frac{3}{4}$ of 20? _____

8. Shade $\frac{1}{3}$ of the shape.

9. Shade $\frac{3}{4}$ of the shape.

   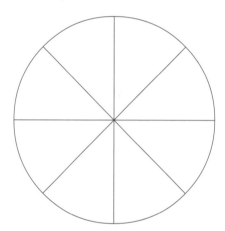

10. Shade and write the equivalent fractions.

    a)

    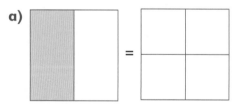

    b) $\frac{1}{2} = \frac{?}{4}$ _____

11. There were 24 cherries on the tree. One quarter of the cherries then fell off on to the ground. How many cherries are on the ground? _____

Score:	Time taken:	Target met?

Target time: **12 minutes**

1. Convert these measurements.

   a) $\frac{1}{2}$ kg = _____ g

   b) $1\frac{1}{2}$ kg = _____ g

   c) $4\frac{1}{2}$ kg = _____ g

   d) $\frac{1}{4}$ m = _____ cm

   e) $1\frac{1}{2}$ m = _____ cm

2. Write these times in words.

   a)

   _____
   _____

   b)
   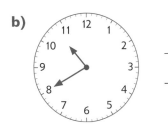
   _____
   _____

   c)
   _____
   _____

   d)
   _____
   _____

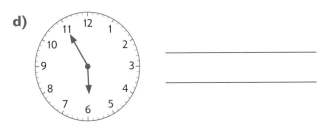

3. It takes me 15 minutes to walk 1km.

   a) How long will it take me to walk 3km? _____ min

   b) If I walk for 1 hour, how far will I have travelled? _____ km

4. Halle's cat weighed $3\frac{1}{2}$ kg. Elsie's cat weighed twice as much. How much did Elsie's cat weigh? _____ kg

5. **Freya's Fruit Shop**

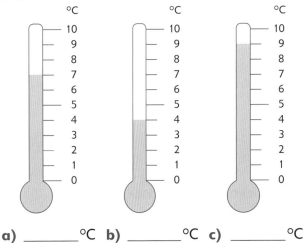

26p   31p   43p   15p

   a) Max buys a pineapple and an apple. How much does he spend? _____ p

   b) Eli buys 2 strawberries and an apple. How much does he spend? _____ p

   c) Ivy buys 3 bananas. How much change does she get from 50p? _____ p

6. What are the temperatures on these thermometers?

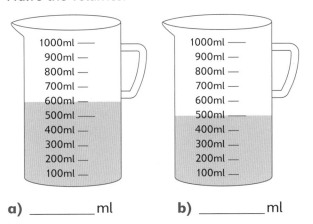

   a) _____ °C b) _____ °C c) _____ °C

7. Halve the volumes.

   a) _____ ml   b) _____ ml

Score: _____   Time taken: _____   Target met? _____

1. Match the 3D shapes to their names and properties.

I have 1 vertex.
I have 1 edge.
I have 2 faces.

cube

I have 8 vertices.
I have 12 edges.
I have 6 faces.

square-based pyramid

I have 0 vertices.
I have 2 edges.
I have 3 faces.

sphere

I have 0 vertices.
I have 0 edges.
I have 1 face.

cone

I have 5 vertices.
I have 8 edges.
I have 5 faces.

2. Name the 2D shapes that make up the faces of these 3D shapes.

a) _____

b) _____

c) _____

d) _____

e) _____

f) _____

3. Draw what these images would look like once they have turned.

a) Make a quarter turn anticlockwise.

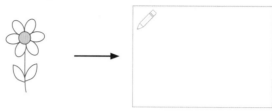

b) Make a three-quarter turn clockwise.

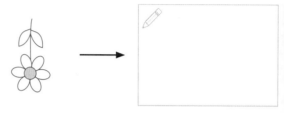

c) Make a half turn clockwise.

4. If you follow these directions, where will the mouse end up? _____

- Go forward 2 squares.

- Turn anticlockwise through 1 right angle.

- Go forward 2 squares.

- Turn clockwise through 1 right angle.

- Go forward 3 squares.

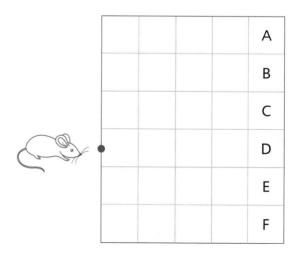

Target time: **12 minutes**

1. This table shows the number of ice lollies sold by a shop one lunchtime.

Flavour	Lemon	Banana	Lime	Cola	Grape
Number sold	12	8	10	5	3

a) Complete the pictogram below.

= 2 ice lollies   = 1 ice lolly

Lemon	
Banana	
Lime	
Cola	
Grape	

b) Which was the most popular flavour of ice lolly?

_____

c) Which was the least popular flavour?

_____

d) The sale of banana ice lollies was equal to the sales of which 2 flavours?

_____

e) How many people bought lime, banana and lemon lollies?   _____

f) The shop started the day with 50 ice lollies. How many were left after lunchtime?   _____

2. Sort these 3D shapes. Write the letters **A**, **B**, **C** and **D** in the correct places in the Venn diagram.

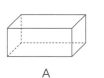

A   B   C   D

Shapes with a rectangular face   Shapes with a triangular face

3. Ty listed each of his friends' favourite fruits.

A O A P C N N S
S O P S A O O C N
O A P C N P S O
A A C C P S N S A

A = Apple
O = Orange
P = Pear
C = Cherry
N = Nectarine
S = Strawberry

Record the information in the tally chart below.

Fruit	Tally	Total
Apple		
Orange		
Pear		
Cherry		
Nectarine		
Strawberry		

Score:		Time taken:		Target met?	

1. A bus seats 47 people. There are 30 empty seats. How many people are on the bus? _____

2. Sweets cost 14p.

   a) Ellie buys 2 sweets. How much does she spend? _____p

   b) How much change does she get from 30p? _____p

3. Write the missing fractions.

   a) _____   b) _____

   c) _____   d) _____

4. Calculate the new prices for these items.

   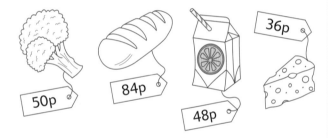

   36p

   84p

   50p

   48p

	Item	Original price	Half price
a)	Broccoli	50p	
b)	Bread	84p	
c)	Orange juice	48p	
d)	Cheese	36p	

5. Solve these calculations.

   a) 26 + 23 =   _____

   b) 58 − 34 =   _____

   c) 10 × 6 =   _____

   d) 40 ÷ 5 =   _____

6. What are the measurements on these scales?

   a)

   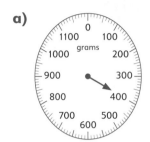

   _____g

   b)

   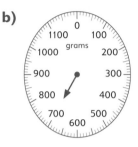

   _____g

7. The block diagram below shows the shoe size of children in Class 2.

   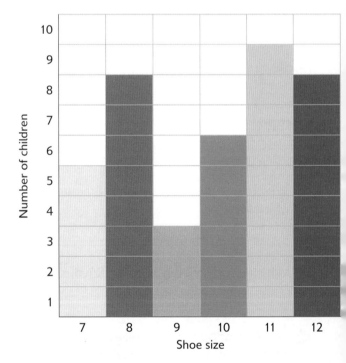

   Shoe sizes of Class 2

   a) How many children had size 9 shoes? _____

   b) Which 2 sizes were the same for an equal number of children? _____

   c) How many children had feet bigger than a size 10? _____

Target time: **12 minutes**

1. Circle the quadrilaterals.

2. Convert the times on the analogue clocks into digital time.

a)

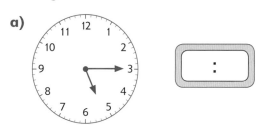

b)

3. Jamie has to walk 2km to school and a further 2km home every weekday. If he does this for a week, how far has he walked? _____ km

4. How much liquid is in each jug?

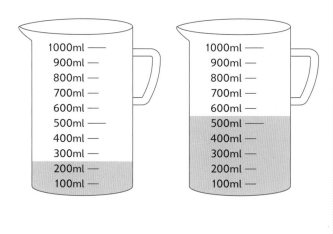

a) _____ ml   b) _____ ml

5. Convert these measurements.

a) 3000ml = _____ l

b) $\frac{1}{2}$l = _____ ml

c) 4l = _____ ml

d) 2500ml = _____ l

6. Shade $\frac{3}{4}$ of these shapes.

a) 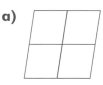   b)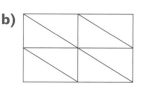

7. Evie has 15 gummy bears. She eats $\frac{1}{3}$ of them. How many has she eaten? _____

8. Tommy has 12 football stickers. He gives $\frac{1}{4}$ away. How many does he keep? _____

9. Draw what these images would look like once they have turned.

a) Make a right-angled turn anticlockwise.

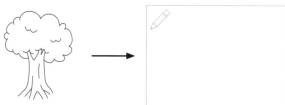

b) Make 3 right-angled turns clockwise.

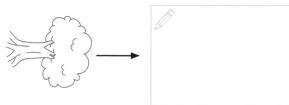

10. Write **<**, **>** or **=** to make these statements correct.

a) 5 × 2 _____ 20 ÷ 2

b) 45 ÷ 5 _____ 2 × 4

c) 4 × 10 _____ 12 × 5

Score: [ ]   **Time taken:** [ ]   **Target met?** [ ]

Target time: **12 minutes**

1. What are the temperatures on these thermometers?

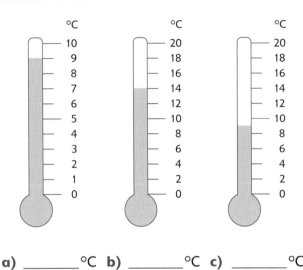

a) _____ °C b) _____ °C c) _____ °C

2. Yasmin swam 25m front crawl, 20m breaststroke and 15m backstroke. How far did Yasmin swim? _____ m

3. Anita thinks of a number. She adds 4 then multiplies by 2. The answer is 14. What was her number? _____

4. Rob thinks of a number. He subtracts 5 then adds 12. The answer is 19. What was his number? _____

5. Write each of these numbers in the correct part of the Carroll diagram.

15, 32, 11, 20, 37, 55, 30, 16

	Multiples of 5	Not multiples of 5
Multiples of 2		
Not multiples of 2		

6. There were 56 children in the playground. Twenty-two more children came outside. How many are in the playground now? _____

7. Write the time 10 minutes earlier and 10 minutes later.

Earlier   **Later**

a) [:] [7:15] b) [:]

c) [:] [4:45] d) [:]

8. Cath went to her friend's house at 5 o'clock. She stayed for an hour.

a) At what time did she leave? _____

b) It took her 30 minutes to get home. At what time did she get home? _____

9. The lion weighs half as much as the elephant. The zebra weighs half as much as the lion. How much do the zebra and lion weigh?

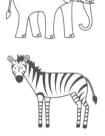

840kg

a) _____ kg

b) _____ kg

10. Mandy bought two books which cost £1.50 each. How much change did she get from £5? £ _____

Score: [ ]   Time taken: [ ]   Target met? [ ]

Target time: **12 minutes**

1. How much liquid is in each container?

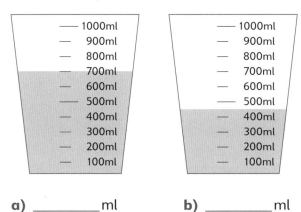

a) _____ ml   b) _____ ml

2. Mark had a plank of wood that was 100cm long. He cut it in half and used one half to make a shelf.

a) How long was the piece of wood he had left?   _____ cm

b) If he cut the remaining piece of wood in half, how long would each piece be?   _____ cm

3. Solve these calculations.

a) If 4 × 7 = 28, then 7 × 4 =   _____

b) If 11 × 4 = 44, then 4 × 11 =   _____

4. Halve and double these numbers.

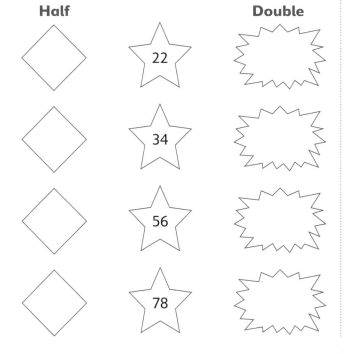

Half   **Double**

22

34

56

78

5. Convert these digital times to analogue by drawing the hands on the clocks.

a) `7:30`

b) `12:15`

6. Audrey made a block diagram to show the types of cat that live in her neighbourhood.

Neighbourhood cats

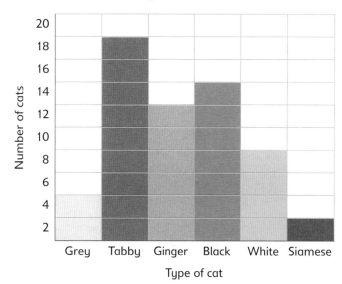

a) What is the second most popular type of cat in Audrey's neighbourhood?

_____

b) What is the least popular type of cat?

_____

c) How many tabby cats live near Audrey?   _____

d) How many cats did Audrey count?   _____

| Score: | | Time taken: | | Target met? | |

Target time: **12 minutes**

1. Solve these calculations.

   a) 20 + _____ = 80

   b) _____ − 7 = 23

   c) 47 + 31 = _____

   d) If 4 × 6 = 24, then 24 ÷ 6 = _____

2. What fraction of each shape is shaded?

   a)

   _____

   b)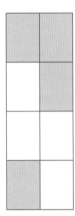

   _____

3. Circle $\frac{3}{4}$ of the fish.

4. There were 38 boxes of cereal on the supermarket shelf. 10 boxes were sold and another 8 boxes were added to the shelf by a member of staff. How many boxes of cereal were on the shelf at the end of the day?

   _____

5. Measure the length of these caterpillars to the nearest $\frac{1}{2}$ cm.

   a)

   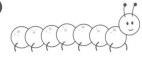

   _____ cm

   b)

   _____ cm

6. Complete the description for each shape.

   a)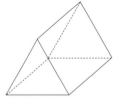

   I have _____ faces.

   I have _____ edges.

   I have _____ vertices.

   I am a _____.

   b)

   I have _____ faces.

   I have _____ edges.

   I have _____ vertices.

   I am a _____.

7. What is 16 multiplied by 2? _____

8. Apples come in bags of 6. If Anya had 5 bags of apples, how many apples did she have altogether? _____

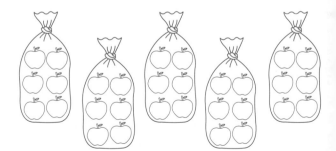

Score:	Time taken:	Target met?

Target time: **12 minutes**

1. Complete these sequences.

a) 6, 9, 12, 15, _____ , _____

b) 34, 29, 24, 19, _____ , _____

c) 66, 76, 86, 96, _____ , _____

2. A group of friends went shopping.

60p

30p

45p

25p

a) Alice bought 2 dolls.
How much did she spend? _____ p

b) Jo bought a doll and a lolly.
How much did she spend? _____ p

c) Simon has 60p. What two different
items could he buy?

_____

d) What would Simon's
change be? _____ p

e) Aziz bought a car and a
teddy. What change did
he get from £1? _____ p

3. Find these lengths.

a) What is $\frac{1}{4}$ of 24cm? _____ cm

b) What is $\frac{2}{4}$ of 34cm? _____ cm

c) What is $\frac{1}{3}$ of 6cm? _____ cm

d) What is $\frac{3}{4}$ of 8cm? _____ cm

4. Gia has 14 toy monsters. She buys
another 12 and is given 6 more.
How many does she have now? _____

5. George shared 55 plums equally
among 5 baskets. How many
plums were in each basket? _____

6. What are the measurements on these scales?

a)

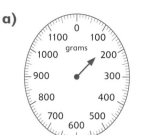

_____ g

b)

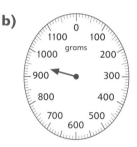

_____ g

7. Look at the grid below.

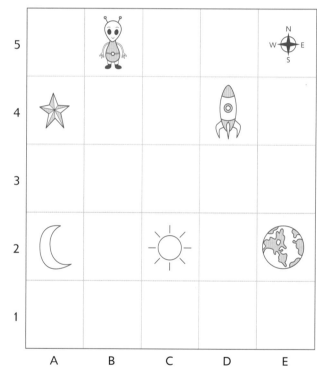

a) What is found in position A4?

_____

b) Where is the alien? _____

c) Which image lies directly to the east of
the moon?

_____

d) Where is the rocket? _____

Score:	Time taken:	Target met?

Progress chart

Write the score (out of 20) for each test in the box provided on the right of the graph.
Then colour in the row next to the box to represent this score.

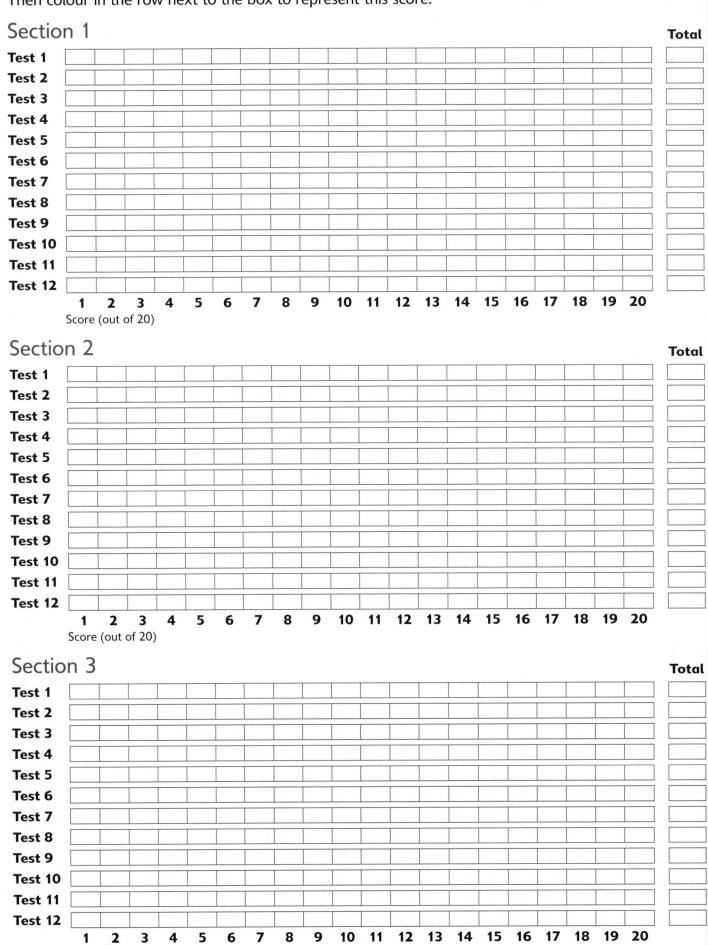

Section 1

Total

Test 1
Test 2
Test 3
Test 4
Test 5
Test 6
Test 7
Test 8
Test 9
Test 10
Test 11
Test 12

1 2 3 4 5 6 7 8 9 10 11 12 13 14 15 16 17 18 19 20
Score (out of 20)

Section 2

Total

Test 1
Test 2
Test 3
Test 4
Test 5
Test 6
Test 7
Test 8
Test 9
Test 10
Test 11
Test 12

1 2 3 4 5 6 7 8 9 10 11 12 13 14 15 16 17 18 19 20
Score (out of 20)

Section 3

Total

Test 1
Test 2
Test 3
Test 4
Test 5
Test 6
Test 7
Test 8
Test 9
Test 10
Test 11
Test 12

1 2 3 4 5 6 7 8 9 10 11 12 13 14 15 16 17 18 19 20
Score (out of 20)